For my year seven science teacher, who told me
to stop doodling in my workbooks . . .

Look at me now, Mrs. Gleeson!

Also, for my mum and dad.

Thanks for not being mad about the

doodles in my workbooks.

**SIMON
ELEMENT**

An Imprint of Simon & Schuster, LLC
1230 Avenue of the Americas
New York, NY 10020

First Simon Element trade paperback edition May 2024

SIMON ELEMENT is a trademark of Simon & Schuster, LLC

Simon & Schuster: Celebrating 100 Years of Publishing in 2024

For information about special discounts for bulk purchases,
please contact Simon & Schuster Special Sales at 1-866-506-1949 or
business@simonandschuster.com.

The Simon & Schuster Speakers Bureau can bring authors
to your live event. For more information or to book an event,
contact the Simon & Schuster Speakers Bureau at 1-866-248-3049 or
visit our website at www.simonspeakers.com.

Manufactured in the United States of America

10 9 8 7 6 5 4 3 2 1

Library of Congress Cataloging-in-Publication Data has been applied for.

ISBN 978-1-6680-5883-1

A DOODLE A DAY KEEPS THE STRESS AWAY

TAMARA MICHAEL

SIMON
ELEMENT

New York   London   Toronto   Sydney   New Delhi

Ultimately, my hope is that this book brings a little peace and calm to your day.

HI, FRIEND!

If you've picked up this book, it's likely that ♡1 you love to draw, or ♡2 you're stressed out, burned out, and looking for a break. If neither of these things are true, then maybe you're just curious, and that's great too. Either way, I'm glad you're here!

This book is not for artists, art critics, or connoisseurs. This book was designed for the stressed out and weary. For the ones who forgot what it was like to draw for no reason and color outside the lines. For anyone tired of staring at their screen, and anyone who misses the feeling of putting pen to paper.

In this book you will find weird and wonderful drawing prompts. Start wherever you like and draw for as long as you need. Starting is always the most difficult part. That's why the first few pages are designed to be easy enough for anyone to try. Don't overthink it; just go with it. No one ever needs to see these drawings, so just allow yourself time and space to be in the moment. I would recommend switching off all devices while you work through your drawing, putting on some calming music, and setting aside a specific time each day to make this a more mindful habit.

DOODLING FUN FACTS

Stress is one of the most common health risks, and can lead to exhaustion, burnout, and a weakened immune system.

Early research suggests that doodling may activate the reward pathways in our brains and reduce stress hormones in our body.

Art can help you navigate complex emotions and feelings that have been repressed in your subconscious.

Research suggests that drawing can help improve your memory.

Drawing can break up the cycle of rumination and interrupt unwanted thoughts.

DOODLING TOOLS

You don't have to have lots of tools—a pencil is all you need. Add color, if you like, with colored pencils and crayons, but no pressure. Pro tip: Test pens and highlighters on the last page of the book to make sure they work well with the paper.

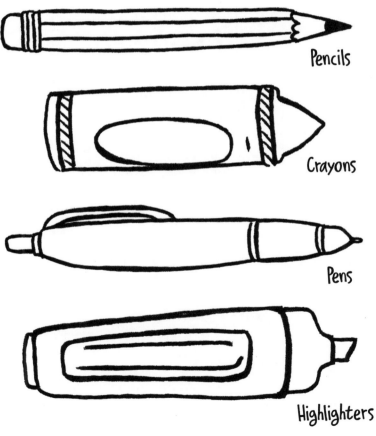

Pencils

Crayons

Pens

Highlighters

PATTERN INSPO

Here are some examples of simple patterns you might like to incorporate into your drawings as you work through this book.

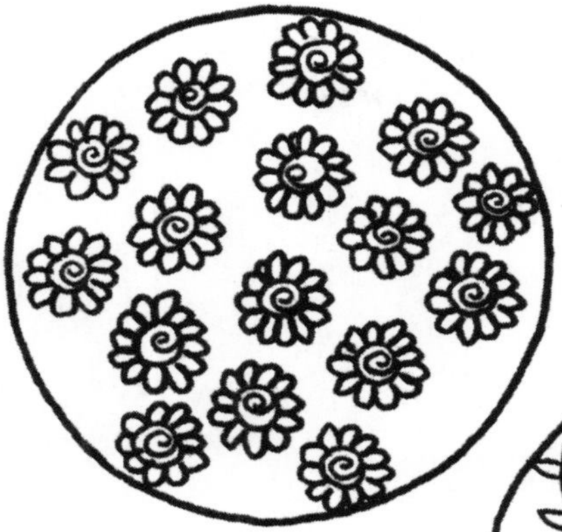
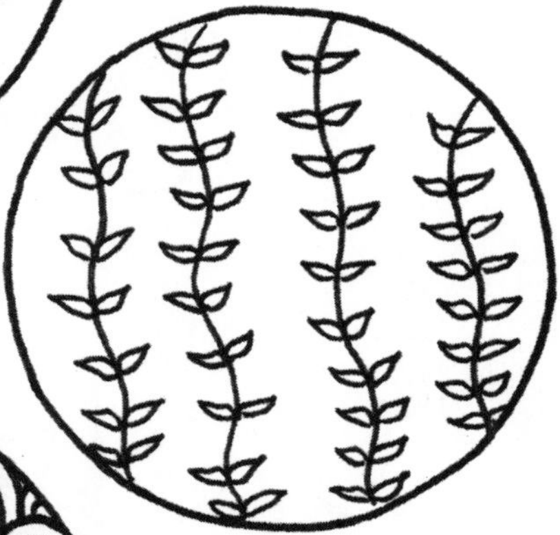
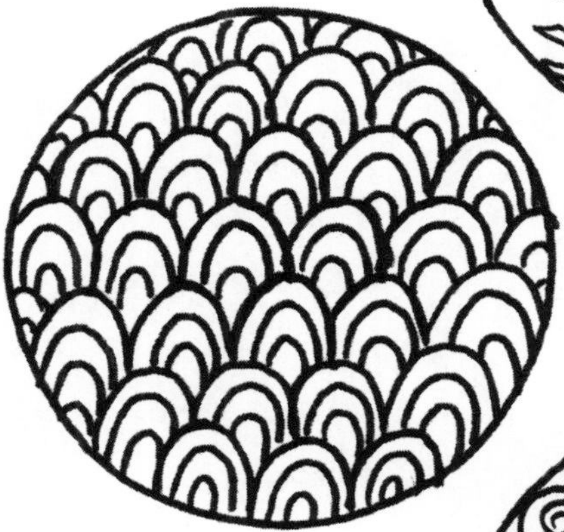
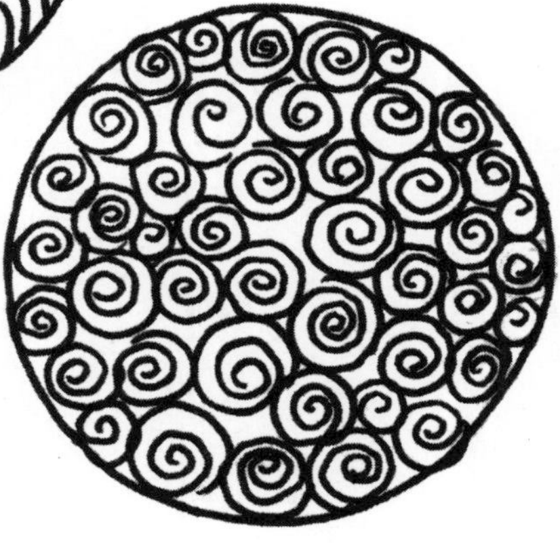

De-stress, one doodle at a time.

FILL THIS PAGE WITH CIRCLES **BIG** AND SMALL.

Doodle square flowers all over the page. Color them in!

DRAW THIS STAR DESIGN IN EACH SQUARE OF THE GRID BELOW.

Use little dots to draw the bee's flight path.

USE THIS SHAPE
TO CREATE A PATTERN.

HINT: FLIP IT, TWIST IT, OVERLAP IT, MAKE IT SMALLER OR LARGER.

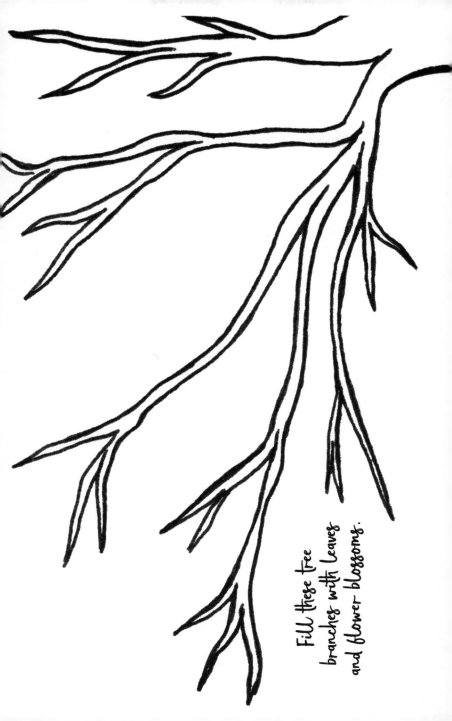

Fill these tree branches with leaves and flower blossoms.

CONTINUE THIS LINE ALL OVER THIS PAGE
WITHOUT LIFTING YOUR PEN.

Continue this design, adding curved lines along each diagonal line.

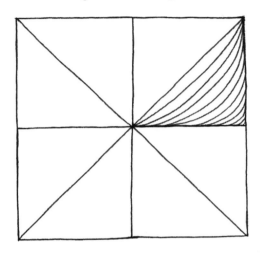

FILL THIS BUCKET TO OVERFLOWING WITH POPCORN.

Use one continuous line to fill
this page with scribbles.

Turn this box into a new wrapping paper design.

DRAW A DIFFERENT FLOWER IN EACH SECTION.

Trace your hand and
design your own jewelry.

COMPLETE THIS PATTERN.

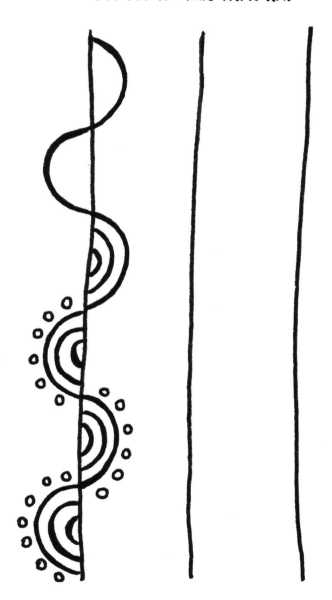

Draw a continuous line of loops and hearts.
Start from the edge of the page and work your way to the center.

COMPLETE EACH LINE.

Fill this page with triangles and squares,
then color them in.

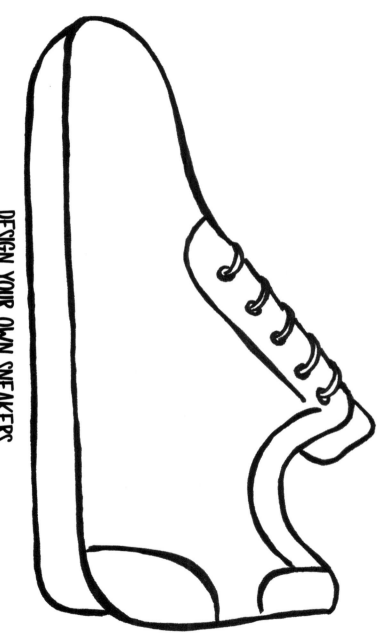

DESIGN YOUR OWN SNEAKERS.

Draw strange and unusual plants in each pot.

FILL EACH CIRCLE WITH A DIFFERENT PATTERN.

Draw a face using one continuous line.

USE A HIGHLIGHTER TO DRAW SQUIGGLES ALL OVER THE PAGE, THEN USE A PEN TO OUTLINE THE EDGES OF THE LINES AND SHAPES.

Fill in this grid with different colors.

Create a pattern.

DRAW DIFFERENT-
SHAPED LEAVES ALL
OVER THIS PAGE.

Draw shooting stars all over this page.

Boost your happy hormones.

DRAW YOUR MORNING COFFEE OR BEVERAGE OF CHOICE.

Draw snow-capped mountains
with a little person at the top.

DRAW LITTLE CRABS ALL OVER THIS PAGE.

Play your favorite song and draw lines, waves, and shapes that represent the music to you.

CONTINUE THIS PATTERN BELOW.

Imagine you're sitting in front of this window. Draw what you see.

WHAT IS INSIDE THIS PACKAGE?

DRAW THE FIRST THING THAT COMES TO MIND.

Draw something that starts with the first letter of your name.

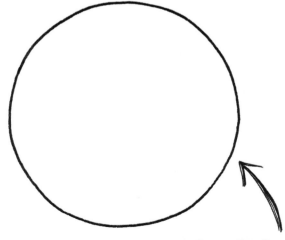

DRAW YOUR FAVORITE MEAL.

Draw **big** and *little* swirls
all over this page.

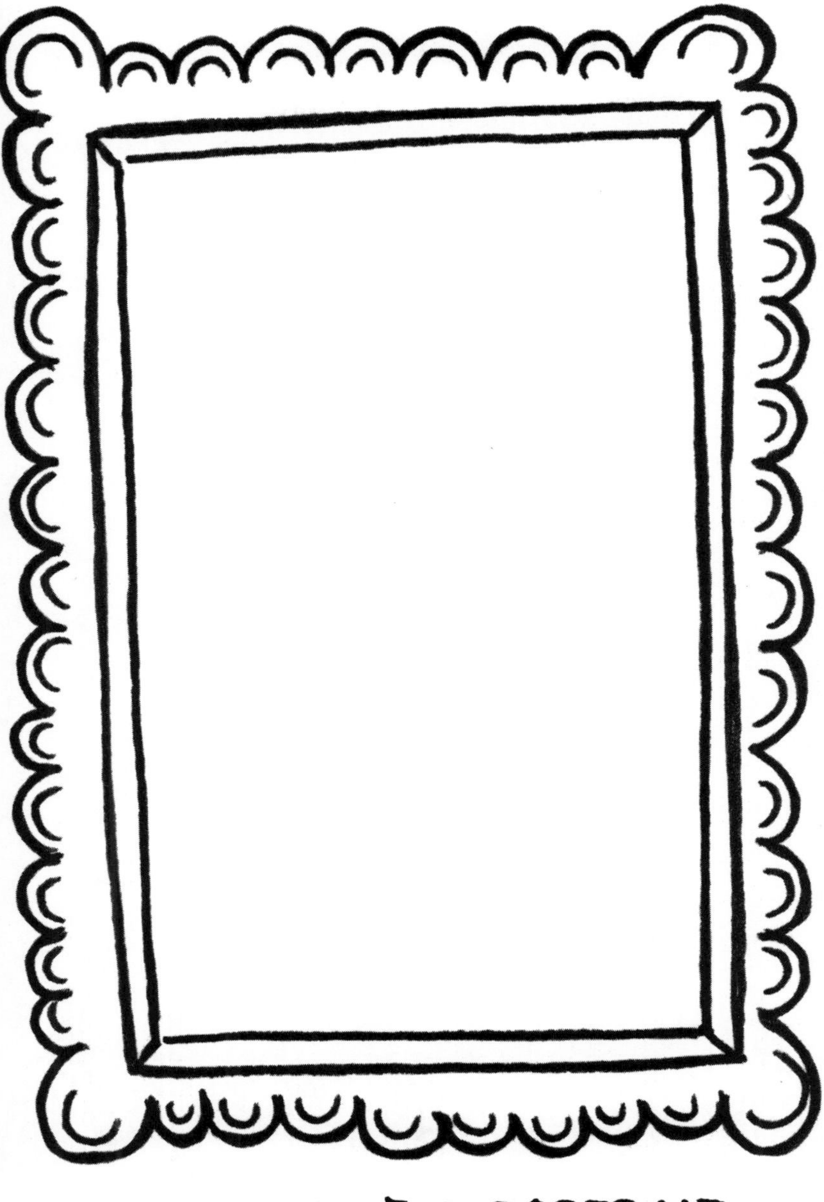

DRAW A SELF-PORTRAIT.

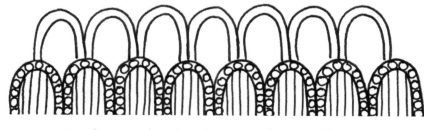

Continue to build up this pattern.

WRITE YOUR NAME IN BUBBLE LETTERS. FILL THE LETTERS AND THE SPACE AROUND THEM WITH PATTERNS.

Fill each wave with a different pattern.

DOODLE ICE CREAM CONES
ALL OVER THIS PAGE.

Design your own crown.

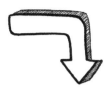

FILL THE SPACE BELOW WITH Xs AND Os.
THEY MUST ALL BE TOUCHING EACH OTHER.

Turn this rectangle into a postcard from somewhere exotic.

Unleash your inner child.

FILL THIS PAGE WITH
COLORFUL POLKA DOTS.

Draw big and small **zigzags** all over this page.

DESIGN A DIFFERENT COVER FOR THIS BOOK.

Look at these squiggles.
What do you see? Draw it.

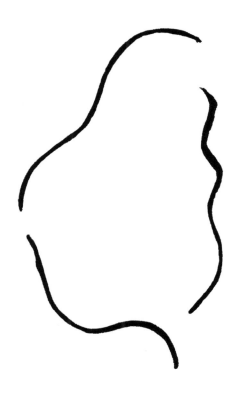

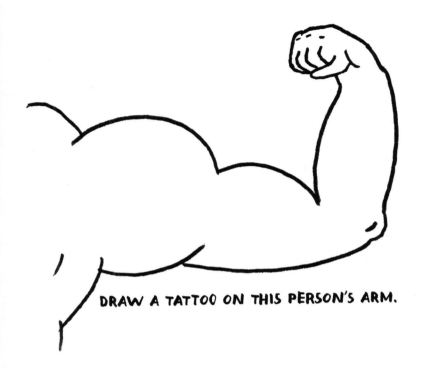

DRAW A TATTOO ON THIS PERSON'S ARM.

Draw the first thing that comes to mind.

FILL THIS PAGE WITH UNUSUAL SHAPES AND BLOBS.

Draw a cactus in this pot.

FEELING ANNOYED? DRAW A PATTERN OR SHAPE THAT REPRESENTS ANGER.

AND BREATHE.

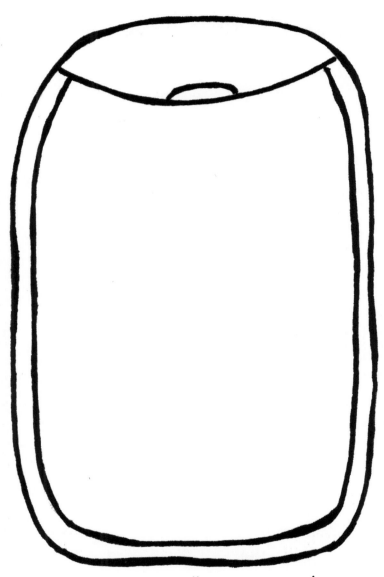

Imagine you're sitting on an airplane.
Draw what you see from your window.

FILL THIS PAGE WITH WAVY LINES.

Draw leaves and flowers
all over these vines.

DRAW AN OUTFIT YOU LOVE WEARING.

Fill this page with tiny daffodils.

DRAW COLORFUL BUNTING HANGING ACROSS THE TOP OF THIS PAGE.

Design the pattern on this butterfly's wings.

NOW DESIGN DIFFERENT WINGS FOR EACH OF THESE BUTTERFLIES.

Fill this page
with spiderwebs.

GIVE THESE
MANNEQUIN
HEADS DIFFERENT
HAIRSTYLES.

Draw overlapping lines all over this page. Fill in each section with more little lines.

FILL THIS TANK WITH LITTLE FISH.

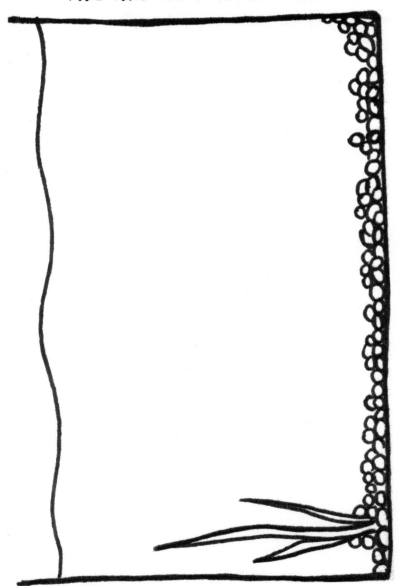

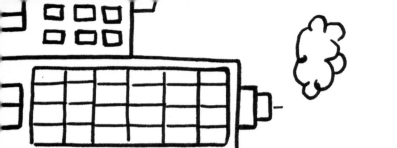

Add more buildings to this cityscape.

DRAW DIFFERENT STYLES OF SUNS. I'VE STARTED ONE FOR YOU.

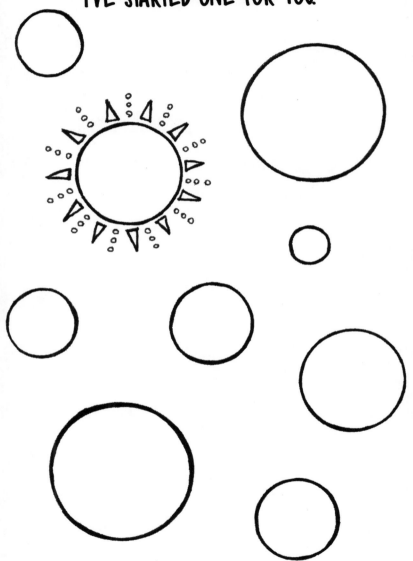

This is
your
reminder
to just
breathe.

Draw your breath. Draw a line up when you inhale and down when you exhale to create your own unique waves across the page.

Feeling anxious? Create a pattern that represents how you feel.

And breathe.

FILL THIS LEAF WITH DIFFERENT PATTERNS.

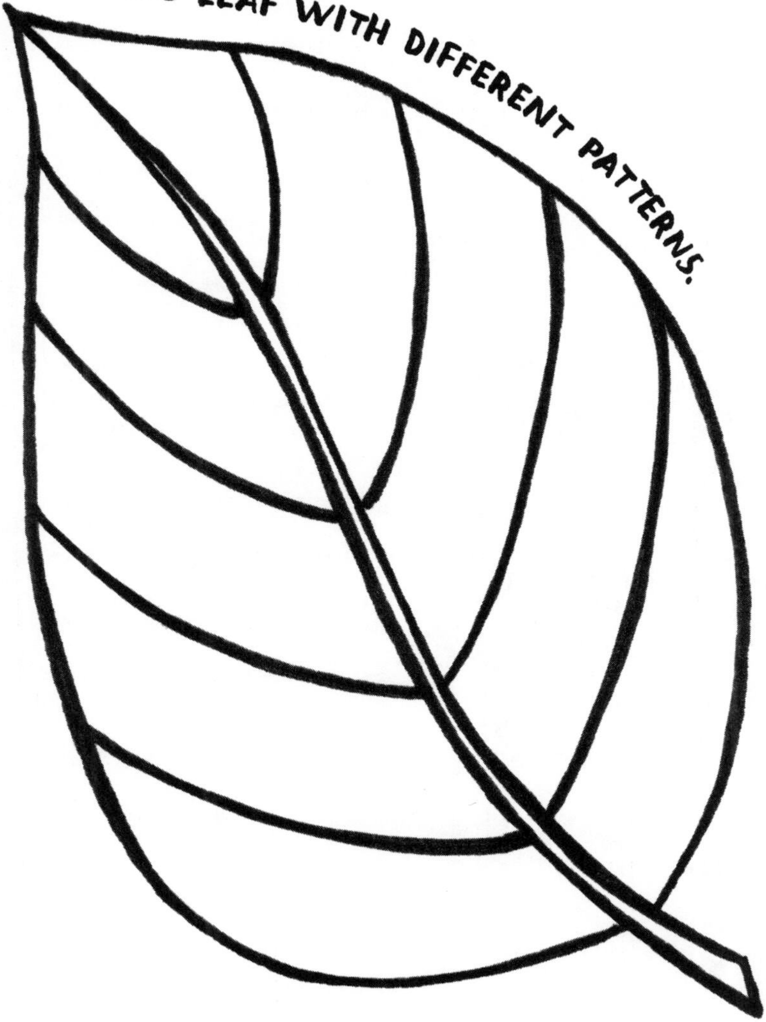

FILL THIS FRIDGE WITH YOUR FAVORITE FOODS.

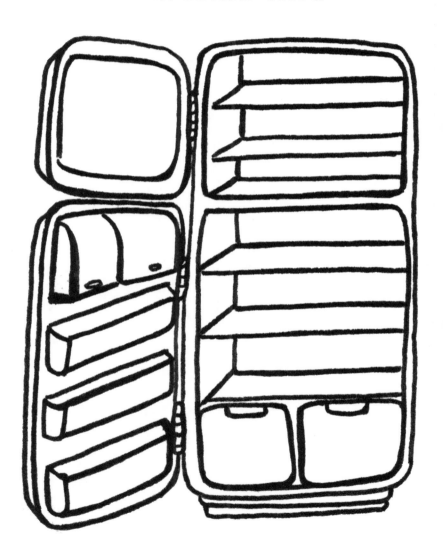

Draw a flower using only triangles.

Complete the pattern.

DRAW LANTERNS BELOW BY CONNECTING THE DOTS WITH CURVED LINES. USE A DIFFERENT COLOR FOR EACH LANTERN.

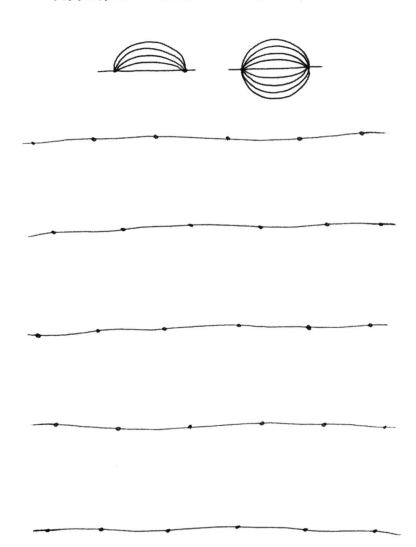

Draw a pattern that represents
calm for you.

**DESIGN A PATTERN
FOR THIS COFFEE MUG.**

Use this shape
to create a pattern.

DRAW JELLYFISH ALL OVER THIS PAGE.

Doodle a house without
lifting your pen from the page.

FILL EACH SECTION WITH A
DIFFERENT SHAPE OR DESIGN.

Trace around the heart. Continue to
draw concentric hearts until you
fill the page. Color in each layer.

DRAW LOOPS ALL OVER THIS PAGE.

Draw a pattern in each feather.

COMPLETE THE PATTERN IN THE GRID BELOW.

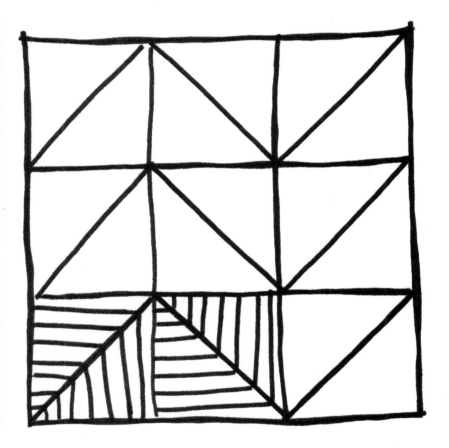

Connect these dots with one continuous line.
Color in or draw patterns in each section.

DOODLE THIS TRIANGLE DESIGN ALL
OVER THE PAGE IN DIFFERENT SIZES.

Express yourself!

Turn these blobs into flowers.

CONTINUE TO DRAW WAVY LINES
AROUND THESE WAVY FLOWERS.
FILL EACH SECTION.

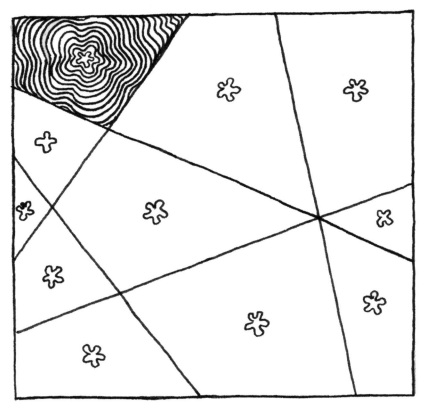

BONUS CHALLENGE: ADD DIFFERENT
COLORS BETWEEN EACH LAYER!

Complete the dandelions.

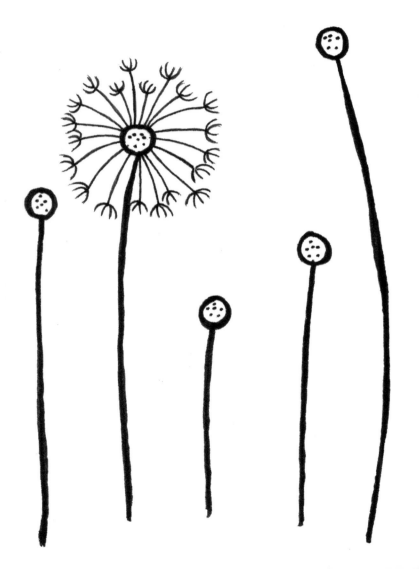

TURN THIS SQUIGGLE INTO A PICTURE.

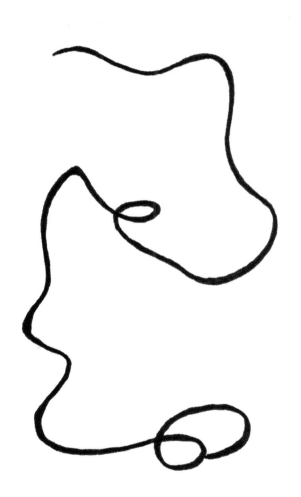

Doodle little cupcakes all over this page.

DRAW WAVES UNDERNEATH THIS TINY BOAT.

Draw rain pouring
over this umbrella.

DOODLE DIFFERENT STYLES OF HOUSE ALL OVER THIS PAGE.

Draw funny-shaped trees
all over this page.

DOODLE LITTLE LOLLIPOPS ALL OVER THIS PAGE.

Complete this design in each square in the grid below.

DRAW THICK AND THIN LINES TO FILL THIS SPACE.

Draw flower petals around this circle.
Start small and gradually get larger and larger.

CREATE A PATTERN WITH THIS SHAPE.

Fill this page with sunflowers.

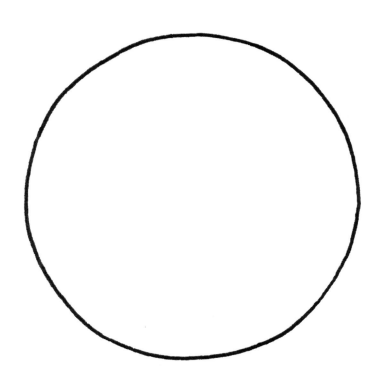

TURN THIS CIRCLE INTO A FLORAL WREATH.

Daily dopamine hit.

FILL THIS PAGE WITH
DIFFERENT SHAPES. DOODLE
PATTERNS IN EACH SHAPE.

Draw faces on these inanimate objects.
Make them silly!

FILL THIS BOWL WITH FRUIT.

Design your ultimate burger.
Label each ingredient.

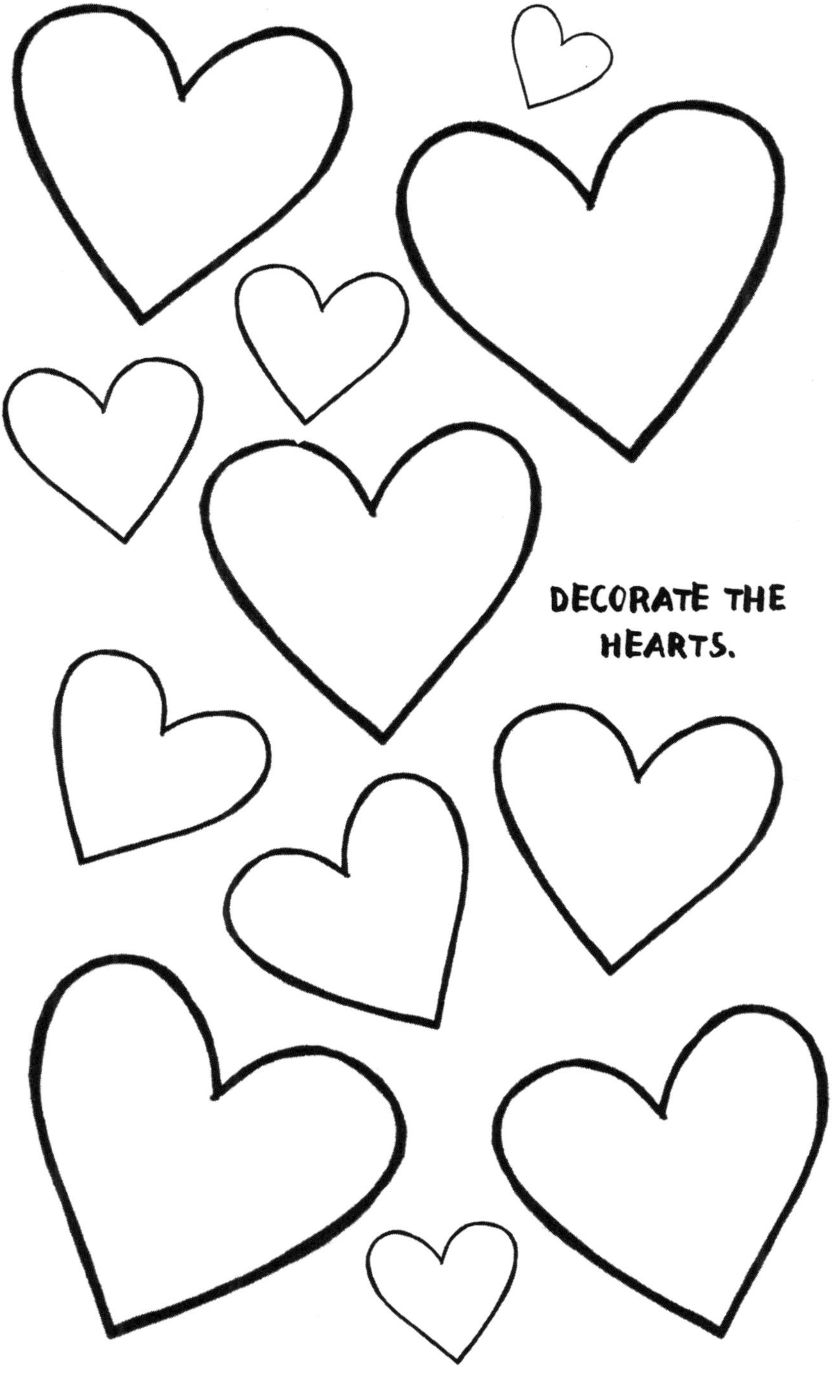

DECORATE THE HEARTS.

Draw as many round things as you can
fit on this page
(such as a pizza, a bagel, and a doughnut).

DESIGN DIFFERENT SYMBOLS FOR EACH LETTER OF THE ALPHABET.

A   B   C   D   E   F   G

H   I   J   K   L   M   N

O   P   Q   R   S   T   U

V   W   X   Y   Z

Continue this figure-eight loop.
Gradually make it larger and larger
until you reach the edges of the page.

DRAW A PATTERN THAT BEST
REPRESENTS HAPPINESS TO YOU.
COLOR IT IN WITH BRIGHT COLORS.

Draw clothes hanging from this clothesline.

DOODLE SEASHELLS ALL OVER THIS PAGE.

Imagine you run your own country. Design the national flag.

DRAW THREE THINGS YOU CAN'T LIVE WITHOUT.

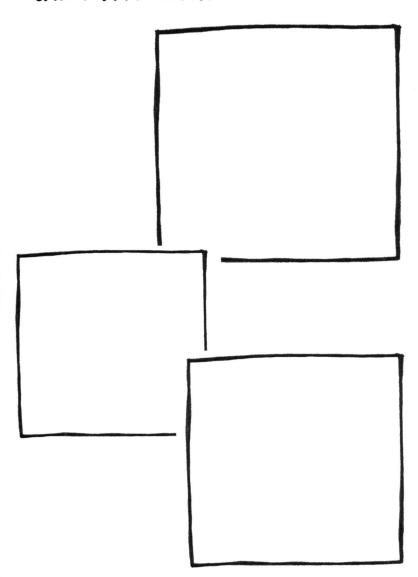

Draw the rings of the tree inside this tree stump.

CONTINUE BUILDING THIS PATTERN.

Design your birthday cake! Be sure to label all the layers and elements of the cake.

TURN THESE TRIANGLES INTO DIFFERENT PARTY HATS.

Clear
your
mind.

Draw something tiny.

DRAW A
FUNKY
PATTERN
ON THESE
SOCKS.

Scribble wildly on this page.

CONTINUE TO ADD LAYERS TO THIS RAINBOW.

Go outside and look at the clouds. Doodle their shapes.

DRAW LITTLE PINEAPPLES ON
RANDOM PAGES OF THIS BOOK.
START WITH A FEW MORE HERE.

Draw something that
reminds you of summer.

USE DIFFERENT COLORS
TO DRAW CONFETTI ALL
OVER THIS PAGE.

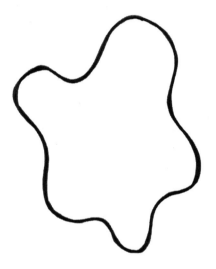

Turn this blob into something.

FILL THIS JAR WITH COLORFUL MARBLES.

DOODLE EYES ALL OVER THIS PAGE.

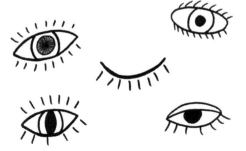

Draw lavender
all over this page.

Draw something you see around you that is blue.

DOODLE DIFFERENT STYLES OF MUSTACHE HERE.

Draw different designs on these hats.

PLAY SOME CALMING MUSIC AND DOODLE
THIS DESIGN ALL OVER THE PAGE.

Design your own currency.

DRAW LITTLE STICK PEOPLE ALL OVER THIS PAGE.

BONUS CHALLENGE: DRAW EACH ONE WITH
DIFFERENT ACCESSORIES, SUCH AS HATS, BAGS, OR SHOES.

Draw your worries away.

ADD A DESIGN
TO THIS T-SHIRT.

Continue building this pattern and color it in.

THIS CHEST HOLDS THE THING YOU TREASURE MOST. DRAW IT.

Draw a shape or pattern that represents freedom.

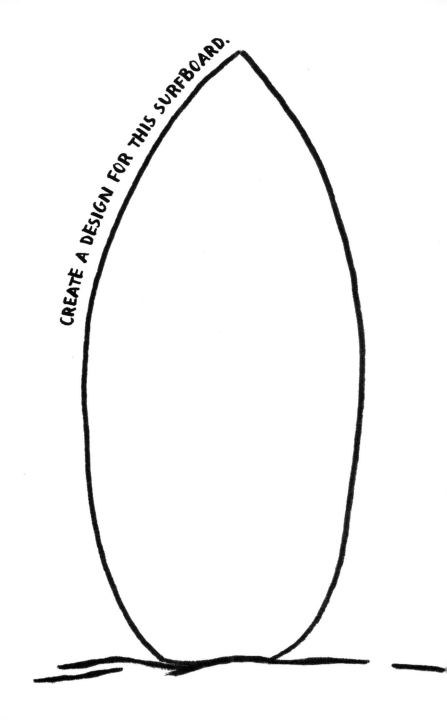

CREATE A DESIGN FOR THIS SURFBOARD.

Doodle little spiders all over this page.

DOODLE THIS FLOWER DESIGN
ALL OVER THE PAGE.

Draw an image in this
Polaroid frame.

DRAW A PATTERN ON
THIS TURTLE'S SHELL.

Draw your favorite pen.

DOODLE A SMALL SNAIL ON THE
FRONT COVER OF THIS BOOK.

Draw a new, undiscovered plant.

DRAW AN APPLE IN EACH CORNER OF THIS PAGE.

Create a geometric pattern in the grid below.

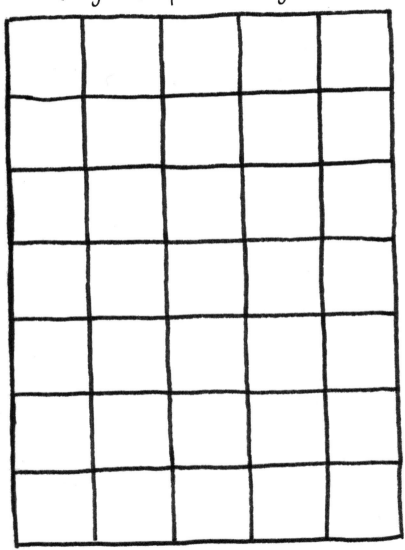

Bonus challenge: Add a color scheme.

CONTINUE TO BUILD THIS CIRCLE OF SQUIGGLES.

DOODLE A
DESIGN ON THIS
SHOPPING BAG.

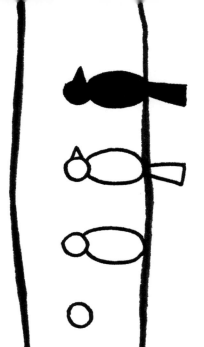

Draw little birds sitting on these wires.

Draw little cats all over this page.

DRAW FACIAL FEATURES AND HAIR ON THIS POTATO.

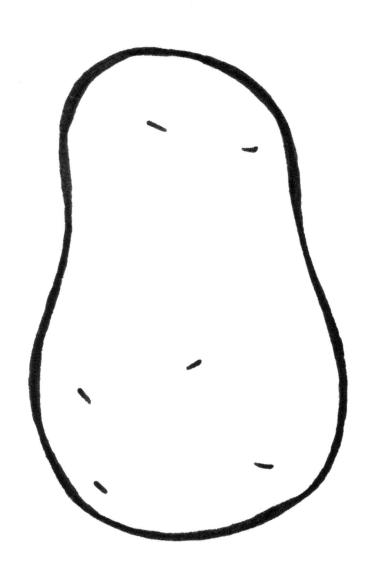

Doodle little raindrops

all

over

this

page.

USE THESE SHAPES
TO CREATE A
WALLPAPER DESIGN
ON THIS PAGE.

Continue to add layers around this spiky shape.
Color in each layer.

DOODLE THIS DESIGN
ALL OVER THIS PAGE
IN DIFFERENT COLORS.

Draw three things that are
in your pocket or bag.

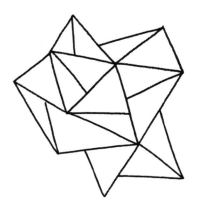

CONTINUE TO BUILD THIS PATTERN,
DRAWING TRIANGLES CONNECTING TO ONE
ANOTHER. COLOR IN EACH TRIANGLE.

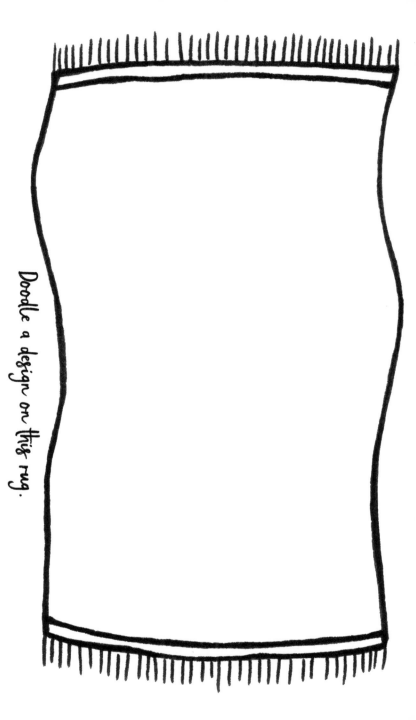

Doodle a design on this rug.

TURN THIS SHAPE INTO A DOUGHNUT WITH SPRINKLES.

Draw tiny ants crawling up this page.

Don't think, just draw.

DRAW FREELY. SHAPES, LINES,
PATTERNS—WHATEVER COMES TO MIND.
DON'T STOP TO THINK ABOUT IT.

Use these three shapes to
design a border for this page.

ASK SOMEONE TO SCRIBBLE HERE.
TURN THAT SCRIBBLE INTO A DRAWING.

Doodle little cows all over this page.

TURN THESE SHAPES INTO BEAUTIFULLY WRAPPED GIFTS.

Doodle fluffy clouds all over this page.

DRAW A BOUQUET OF TWELVE LONG-STEMMED ROSES.

Doodle patterns inside
each of these stars.

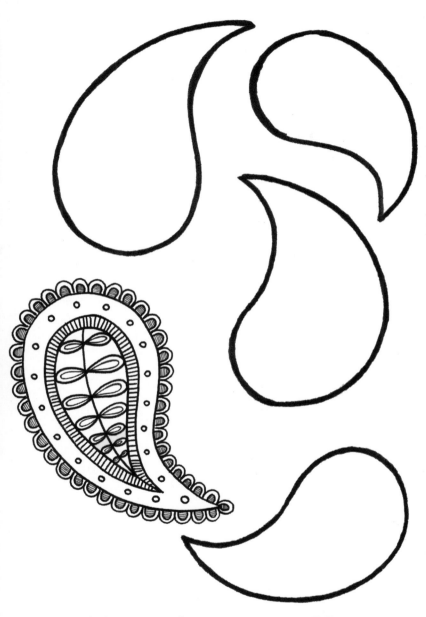

DECORATE THESE SHAPES
WITH PAISLEY PATTERNS.

Create a connect-the-dots drawing and ask someone else to complete it.

DRAW LITTLE LADYBUGS ALL OVER THIS PAGE.

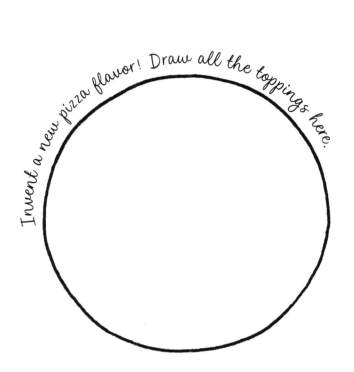

Invent a new pizza flavor! Draw all the toppings here.

DRAW SOMETHING THAT REPRESENTS LOVE TO YOU.

Doodle rocket ships and UFOs all over this page.

START IN THE CENTER AND DRAW
A TINY SHAPE—ANY SHAPE.
DRAW OUTLINES AROUND THAT SHAPE UNTIL
YOU'VE FILLED THE ENTIRE PAGE.

FOR EXTRA FUN, ADD A PATTERN TO EACH LAYER.

Draw a hat, mittens, and a scarf on this penguin.

 DRAW A BORDER OF
WATERMELON SLICES
AROUND THIS PAGE.

Doodle mushrooms of all shapes and sizes here.

DRAW THE FIRST THING THAT COMES TO MIND STARTING WITH THE LETTER H.

Draw a genie coming
out of this lamp.

DESIGN DIFFERENT STYLES OF SUNGLASSES.

Time to release your anxious thoughts.

Fill these circle flowers with different patterns.

DESIGN DIFFERENT STYLES OF SNOWFLAKE.

Draw a sun with wavy rays of light that stretch to the edges of the box.

DESIGN A NEW EMOJI.

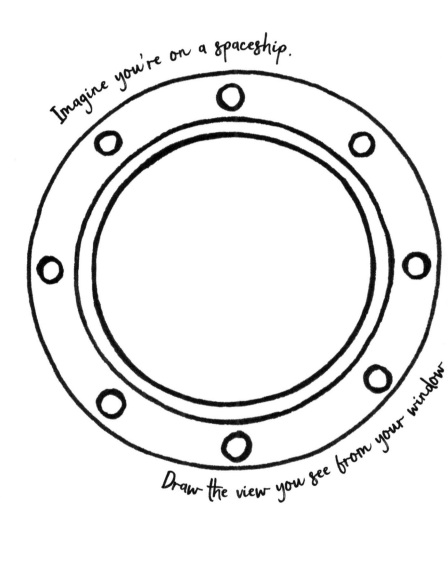

Imagine you're on a spaceship.

Draw the view you see from your window

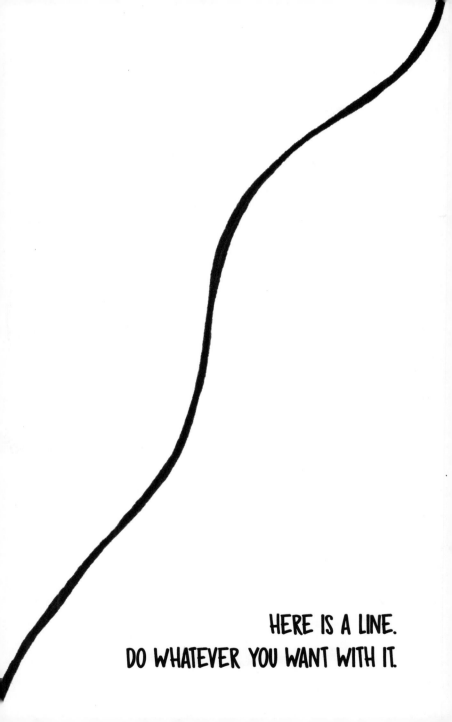

HERE IS A LINE.
DO WHATEVER YOU WANT WITH IT.

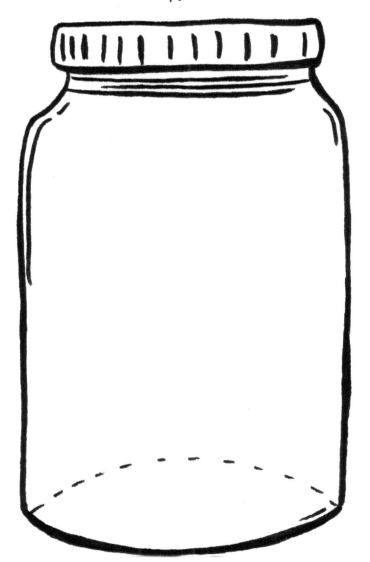

Fill this jar with little fireflies.

DESIGN A TREASURE MAP.

Design a pattern for this quilt.

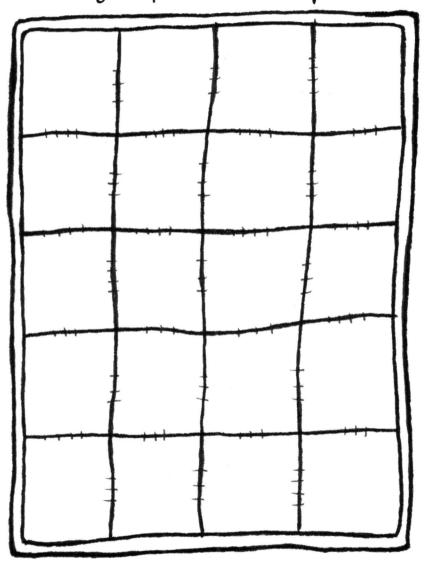

DRAW COLORED JELLY BEANS ALL OVER THE PAGE.

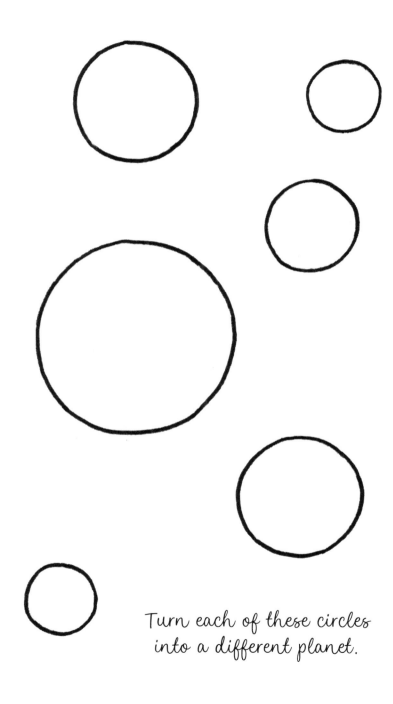

Turn each of these circles into a different planet.

DRAW DIFFERENT-SHAPED BALLOONS ON STRINGS.

Doodle different vegetables across the page.

DRAW A DESIGN ON THIS LAMPSHADE.

Draw four-leaf clovers
all over this page.

IMAGINE THE SQUARES BELOW ARE
THE WINDOWS OF AN APARTMENT BUILDING.
DRAW PEOPLE DOING DIFFERENT THINGS
IN EACH OF THE WINDOWS.

Give this giraffe a pattern other than spots.

FILL THIS PAGE
WITH BUBBLES.

Draw little turtles walking
along the edges of this page.

**DOODLE VINES
ALL AROUND THIS
SENTENCE.**

Doodle this shape all over the page.
Bonus challenge: Try to connect them!

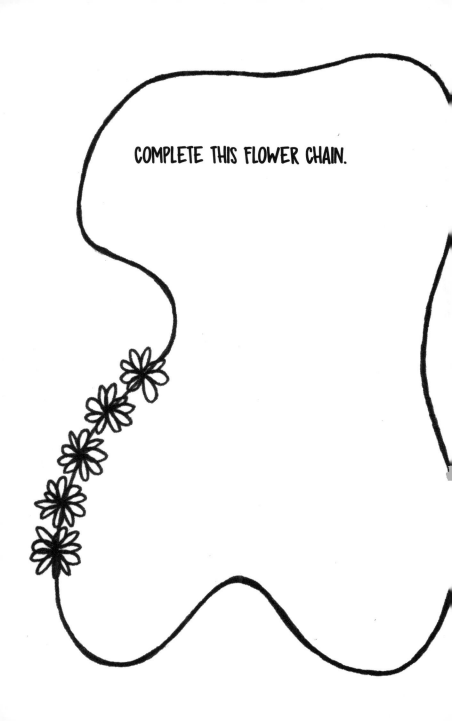

COMPLETE THIS FLOWER CHAIN.

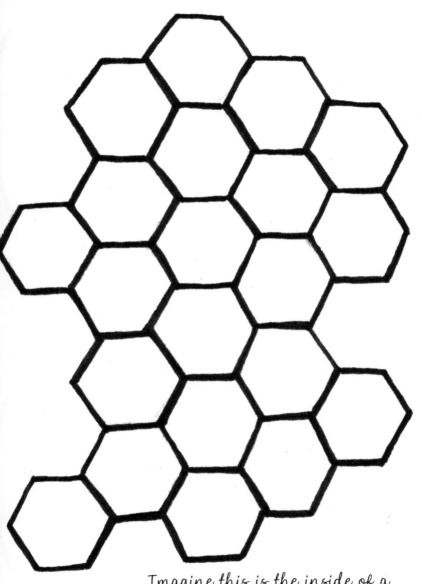

Imagine this is the inside of a
beehive. Draw bees hard at work.

CREATE A PATTERN USING ONLY NUMBERS.

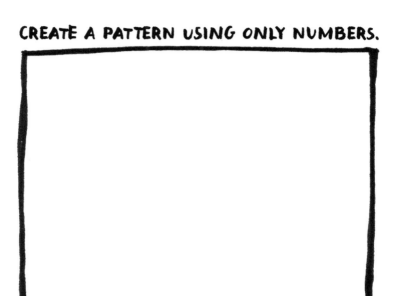

Draw a tiny person wearing a sombrero in the corner of this page.

DRAW DIAMONDS ALL OVER THIS PAGE.

Draw a track of little paw prints on this page.

DRAW DIFFERENT-
SHAPED KITES FLYING
ALL OVER THIS PAGE.

Draw a strange-looking door
that leads to another world.

DRAW AN IMAGE OR PATTERN THAT REPRESENTS HOW YOU'RE FEELING RIGHT NOW.

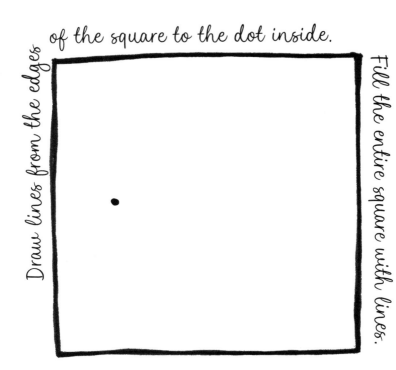

Draw lines from the edges of the square to the dot inside.

Fill the entire square with lines.

WRITE YOUR NAME IN MANY DIFFERENT styles AND fonts.

Fill this jar with different types of colorful candy.

DRAW DIFFERENT-SIZED FIREWORKS ALL
OVER THIS SPACE. USE LOTS OF COLORS!

Copy this pattern in the zigzag lines below.

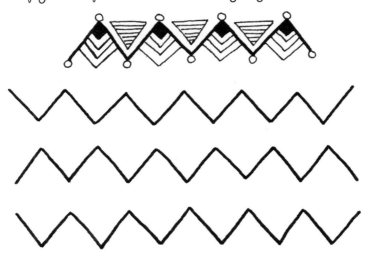

DRAW THIS DESIGN IN THE SQUARE BELOW.

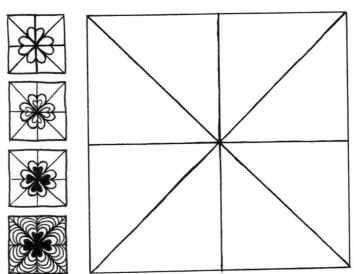

Look away from your screen.

Doodle more triangles with funky designs.
Color them in.

DESIGN AN UGLY SWEATER.

Draw this design in each square of the grid below.

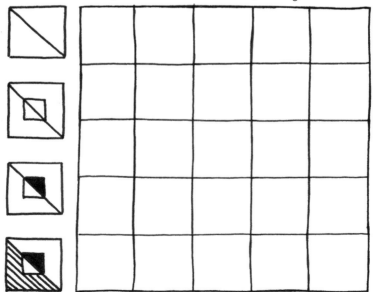

CONTINUE THE DESIGN IN EACH BLOB.

Use this space to doodle during a meeting, a lon

phone call, or while listening to an audiobook.

SCAN THIS IMAGE
FOR MORE DOODLE INSPIRATION
FROM TAMARA MICHAEL